Like a Beggar

ALSO BY ELLEN BASS

POETRY

The Human Line

Mules of Love

No More Masks! An Anthology of Poems by Women, coedited with Florence Howe

NONFICTION

Free Your Mind: The Book for Gay, Lesbian and Bisexual Youth—and Their Allies,
coauthored with Kate Kaufman

*Beginning to Heal: A First Book for Men and Women Who Were Sexually Abused as
Children,* coauthored with Laura Davis

The Courage to Heal: A Guide for Women Survivors of Child Sexual Abuse,
coauthored with Laura Davis

I Never Told Anyone: Writings by Women Survivors of Child Sexual Abuse,
coedited with Louise Thornton and others

CHILDREN'S BOOKS

I like you to make jokes with me, but I don't want you to touch me

Ellen Bass
Like a Beggar

COPPER CANYON PRESS

PORT TOWNSEND, WASHINGTON

Cover art: Carolyn Watts, *CLA* (detail), 2004. Oil and charcoal on canvas, 72 x 72 in.

Copper Canyon Press is in residence at Fort Worden State Park in Port Townsend, Washington, under the auspices of Centrum. Centrum is a gathering place for artists and creative thinkers from around the world, students of all ages and backgrounds, and audiences seeking extraordinary cultural enrichment.

LIBRARY OF CONGRESS CATALOGING-IN-PUBLICATION DATA

Bass, Ellen.
  [Poems. Selections]
  Like a beggar / Ellen Bass.
     pages cm
  ISBN 978-1-55659-464-9 (PBK.)
  I. TITLE.
  PS3552.A817A6 2014
  811'.54—dc23
                    2013036863

COPPER CANYON PRESS
Post Office Box 271
Port Townsend, Washington 98368
www.coppercanyonpress.org

ACKNOWLEDGMENTS

Grateful acknowledgment is made to the following publications where these poems or previous versions of them first appeared.

The Academy of American Poets Poem-A-Day: "Waiting for Rain"

The American Poetry Review: "The Beginning of the End," "Cold," "Looking at a *Diadegma insulare* Wasp under a Microscope," "Nakedness," "Ode to Dr. Ladd's Black Slit Skirt," "Ordinary Sex," "Relax," "Their Naked Petals," "Walking by Circle Market Late at Night," "Women Walking," "The World Has Need of You"

The Missouri Review: "Jazz," "The Last Week" (originally titled "Surrender"), "Ode to Boredom"

Narrative: "Another Story," "French Chocolates," "Let's," "Ode to Repetition," "Prayer"

New Ohio Review: "The Muse of Work"

The New Republic: "When You Return"

The New Yorker: "The Morning After," "What Did I Love"

Orion: "Ode to the Fish," "Saturn's Rings"

Ploughshares: "Restaurant"

Plume: "Deceiving the Gods"

Poet Lore: "Morning"

Poetry Northwest: "Boat, Vietnam," "Pleasantville, New Jersey, 1955"

Prairie Schooner: "Cheetah," "Ode to Invisibility," "Reading Neruda's 'Ode to the Onion'"

The Progressive: "Flies," "Ode to the Heart"

Rattle: "How I Became Miss America"

Red Wheelbarrow: "Bottom Line," "Soixante-Neuf"

Solo Novo: "More"

The Sun: "At the Padre Hotel in Bakersfield, California," "Ode to the God of Atheists"

Tin House: "Moth Orchids," "Ode to the First Peach"

upstreet: "Neighbor"

Zeek: "Moonlight"

Thank you to the Virginia Center for the Creative Arts for the time and space to write. To Toi Derricotte, Lucy Diggs, Frank Gaspar, Marie Howe, Danusha Laméris, Kim Rosen, Clare Wesley, Michael Wiegers, and Cecilia Woloch, thank you for generous and insightful comments. Thank you to Charlotte Raymond for your faithful support. Thank you to my students for all you teach me. Janet Bryer, my haven, my heart, thank you for being by my side through it all. And to Dorianne Laux and Joe Millar, there are no thanks sufficient, but my gratitude is forever.

for Dorianne Laux

But those dark, deadly, devastating ways,

how do you bear them, suffer them?

—I praise.

Rainer Maria Rilke

CONTENTS

Like a Beggar

Relax

Bad things are going to happen.
Your tomatoes will grow a fungus
and your cat will get run over.
Someone will leave the bag with the ice cream
melting in the car and throw
your blue cashmere sweater in the dryer.
Your husband will sleep
with a girl your daughter's age, her breasts spilling
out of her blouse. Or your wife
will remember she's a lesbian
and leave you for the woman next door. The other cat—
the one you never really liked—will contract a disease
that requires you to pry open its feverish mouth
every four hours. Your parents will die.
No matter how many vitamins you take,
how much Pilates, you'll lose your keys,
your hair, and your memory. If your daughter
doesn't plug her heart
into every live socket she passes,
you'll come home to find your son has emptied
the refrigerator, dragged it to the curb,
and called the used-appliance store for a pickup—drug money.
The Buddha tells a story of a woman chased by a tiger.
When she comes to a cliff, she sees a sturdy vine
and climbs halfway down. But there's also a tiger below.
And two mice—one white, one black—scurry out
and begin to gnaw at the vine. At this point
she notices a wild strawberry growing from a crevice.
She looks up, down, at the mice.
Then she eats the strawberry.
So here's the view, the breeze, the pulse
in your throat. Your wallet will be stolen, you'll get fat,
slip on the bathroom tiles in a foreign hotel

and crack your hip. You'll be lonely.
Oh, taste how sweet and tart
the red juice is, how the tiny seeds
crunch between your teeth.

Saturn's Rings

Last night I saw the rings of Saturn
for the first time, that brilliant band
of icy crystals and dust. Mirrors
shepherding the light, collecting it
like pollen or manna
or pails of sweet clear water drawn
from the depths of an ancient well.
The gleam poured through my pupils
into this small, temporary body,
my wrinkled brain in its eggshell skull,
my tunneling blood, breasts that remember
the sting and flush of milk.
Saturn, its frozen rings fire-white,
reflecting the sun from a billion miles.
Maybe there's a word in another language
for when distance dissolves into time.
How are we changed when we stand out
under the fat stars of summer,
our pores opening in the night?
The earth from Saturn is a pale blue orb,
smaller than the heart of whomever you love.
You don't forget the poles of the earth
turning to slush,
you don't forget the turtles
burning in the gulf.
Burger King at the end of the block
is frying perfectly round patties,
the cows off I-5 stand ankle-deep
in excrement. The television
spreads its blue wings over the window
of the house across the street
where someone's husband pressed a gun
against the ridged roof of his mouth.

This choreography of ruin, the world breaking
like glass under a microscope,
the way it doesn't crack all at once
but spreads out from the damaged cavities.
Still, for a moment, it all recedes.
The backyard potatoes swell quietly,
buried beneath their canopy of leaves.
The wind rubs its hands through the trees.

Reading Neruda's "Ode to the Onion"

My son brings the poem to his farm crew
gathered with coffee in the makeshift lean-to, 7 a.m.,
the sun already at its green work, and they don't believe it
when Neruda says the onion is *more beautiful*
than a bird of dazzling feathers… heavenly globe…
dance of the snowy anemone.

These young people bury the black seeds.
Weed, water, watch over them,
then pull the fat bulbs from sweet dirt.
I've seen my son walk the rows,
nudging the drip hose over the small shoulder
of soil toward the stem of a plant.

I say, long live their insistence on reality.
May they always muddy their hands in the actual,
handle the hard evidence of the earth.

But if Neruda could stretch the accordion of time,
he'd explain that when he says he loves the onion
more than the birds, it doesn't mean
he loves the birds less.

When he thinks of the onion, there is nothing
but onion-ness, translucent sleeves that give way
to only themselves. When he praises the onion,
nothing else exists, like nothing else exists
in the center of the onion. Like nothing else exists
when you fall in love.

The rest of the world goes silent.
For a while.

And then the earth starts to turn again.

Seasons reappear.
You get hungry and want a sandwich.
One day you read a book.
You may even fall in love with someone else.

The great ones regard every moment like this,
catch it as it swims—onion, bird, flower, fish—
the way a bear scoops a salmon from the river.
They love the oily orange flesh and the fins,
the pewter eye, the slimy entrails, and the harp of bones.
The masters eat everything right up to their death.
And then they grab that, too, in their failing fist.

At the Padre Hotel in Bakersfield, California

It's Saturday night and all the heterosexuals
in smart little dresses and sport coats
are streaming into what we didn't know
was the hottest spot between Las Vegas and L.A.
Janet and I are in jeans and fleece—not a tube of lipstick
or mascara wand between us. Grayheads:
a species easy to identify without a guidebook—
the over-the-hill lesbian couples of the Pacific Northwest.
Janet's carrying our red-and-white cooler with snacks for the road
across the marble tiles of the Art Deco lobby
when we turn and see the couple
entering through the tall glass doors, slicing
through the crowd like a whetted blade. The butch
is ordinary enough, a stocky white woman
in tailored shirt and slacks, but the confection—
no, the pièce de résistance—whose hand she holds
is of another genus entirely.
Her cinnamon sheen, her gold dress
zipped tighter than the skin of a snake.
And her deep décolletage, exposed enough for open-heart surgery.
She's a yacht in a sea of rowboats.
An Italian fountain by Bernini.
She's the Statue of Liberty. The Hubble Telescope
that lets us gaze into the birth of galaxies.
Oh, may they set that hotel room ablaze—here
in this drab land of agribusiness and oil refineries
outdoing Pittsburgh as the top polluted city in the nation—trash it
like rock stars, rip up the 300 thread-count sheets,
free the feathers from the pillows.
And may that grande femme be consumed
right down to the glitter on her sling-back four-inch stilettos
and whatever she's glued on her magnificent skin
to keep the plunge of that neckline from careening clear off the curve.

Nakedness

The first time I saw my boyfriend's penis,
I thought the shaft would be covered with hair,

like the grassy knoll of my own sex.
My grandmother plucked the last feathers

off the capon, its skin slippery, follicles
little crater-shaped bumps. I once wrung

the neck of a baby bird fallen from its nest,
a shard of shell stuck to its down. Nakedness

of the newborn, smeared with vernix and blood,
splayed like a frog on the sunken belly of the mother,

the tough, swirled cord pulsing. Nakedness
of my mother's body cooling, blood receding

from her nail beds, fingers turning ivory. After death,
the jaw falls open, exposing the naked tongue, dry

and prickled as a cactus paddle. When the Torah
is lifted from the ark, it's an honor to take off

its silver crown and breastplate, velvet cloak and robe.
After the day's portion is read, it's an honor to dress

the naked Word again. Laura shaved her head
so she wouldn't have to watch her hair fall prey

to the teeth of the comb, a pool on her pillow.
Manet painted *Luncheon on the Grass*, cherries

and yellow pears tumbling from the basket.
The two men are dressed, complete with ties

and coats, the woman is naked. In the seventies
Marabel Morgan advised wives

to greet their husbands at the door bound
in Saran Wrap. I knew a woman who liked

to clean house naked. If someone rang the bell,
even a pair of Jehovah's Witnesses in white shirts

and black laced shoes, she answered it like that.
It was her house, she said. My husband was

her husband's therapist. When her husband
killed himself, my husband quit his practice.

That was long ago, my ex-husband's dead, too.
When we were married he wanted me to sleep naked.

I said my shoulders got cold. So he took my
flannel nightgown and cut it off under the armpits.

We laughed so hard you'd have thought
we'd stay together. Once I passed a woman

hiking in the hills of Santa Cruz, naked
except for white athletic shoes. When my children

were small they loved to be naked. My son
stood on his chair at the dinner table, his tiny penis

poised above his plate. I was in a hotel in Missouri
flipping through the stations on TV. Half the shows

were women flashing their breasts, jamming
themselves in front of the camera or on all fours

being fucked from behind. The other half were
fundamentalists ranting against them. I love to lie

down next to Janet's naked body. Her heat
is the closest thing I know to the sun.

So many years ago we rolled naked
down the dunes in Death Valley. The perfect

cones of her breasts, dusted with grains of sand.
When Eleanor's daughter could not recover,

her heart was lifted out of her chest, cupped
naked in the air, and planted in a Chilean

businessman. Years later, when they met
and embraced, she felt her daughter's heart

beating against her breast. The nakedness of houses
when people have moved out, square shadows

where pictures once hung, dusty pennies,
paperclips, insect carcasses. Sacramento

red-brown dirt without rice shoots or walnut trees,
waiting naked for the next crop of shopping malls.

Naked hunger. Naked fear. When you look into a face
and see the need, naked as peeled fruit. Naked prayer

you don't believe in, but pray anyway
because you can't help it, naked, stupid

in your hope. Your daughter is dancing in a cage,
her naked thighs that once pushed out between

your naked thighs now wrap around a silver pole
while men hold their naked hunger in their naked

palms to escape their naked pain. But you can't stop
thinking about her naked toes the first time you

took her to the sea.

Moth Orchids

If you are ill or can't sleep, you can
watch them spread their wings—the hours
it might take for a baby to be born—
the furled sepals arching, until
the petals splay like a woman stretched, flung
open, blood blooming through her veins.
And then stillness, the white fans glisten
day after day like sunlit snow
tinged with a greeny kiss.
Intricate, curved labellum like bones
of a tiny pelvis and the slender tongue reaching out
to the air as though the parts of the body
could blend: mouth fused to hips, face to sex,
the swollen pad where the bee lands.
Here they float:
eleven creamy moths, eleven white egrets
suspended in flight, eleven babies in satin bonnets,
eleven brides stiff in lace, the waxy pools
of eleven white candles, eleven planets
burning in space.

Ode to Repetition

I like to take the same walk
down the wide expanse of Woodrow to the ocean,
and most days I turn left toward the lighthouse.
The sea is always different. Some days dreamy,
waves hardly waves, just a broad undulation
in no hurry to arrive. Other days the surf's drunk,
crashing into the cliffs like a car wreck.
And when I get home I like
the same dishes stacked in the same cupboards
and then unstacked and then stacked again.
And the rhododendron, spring after spring,
blossoming its pink ceremony.
I could dwell in the kingdom of Coltrane,
those rivers of breath through his horn,
as he forms each phrase of "Lush Life"
over and over until I die. Once I was afraid
of this, opening the curtains every morning,
only to close them again each night.
You could despair in the fixed town of your own life.
But when I wake up to pee, I'm grateful
the toilet's in its usual place, the sink with its gift of water.
I look out at the street, the halos of lampposts
in the fog or the moon rinsing the parked cars.
When I get back in bed I find
the woman who's been sleeping there
each night for thirty years. Only she's not
the same, her body more naked
in its aging, its disorder. Though I still
come to her like a beggar. One morning
one of us will rise bewildered
without the other and open the curtains.
There will be the same shaggy redwood
in the neighbor's yard and the faultless stars
going out one by one into the day.

Looking at a *Diadegma insulare* Wasp under a Microscope

It's cleaning its head,
using both appendages,
running them from what would be the nape

of its neck up over the crown
and down its face, not unlike a person
drying after a shower or a swim. The gesture

so familiar, in spite of the exotic cranium,
round and shiny as a pearl of caviar
and overwhelmed by two huge eyes,

more like shields, carmine red
with evenly spaced black dots.
The wasp swivels its head

on a neck thin as sewing thread.
And of course there are the wings
with their unique venation,

the segmented antennae,
and barbed legs, the feet
with their twin splayed tarsi,

and that wasp waist, shocking
how anything that slender
could conduct the business of life.

All the while the thorax is expanding
and contracting, making me aware
of my own shallow breath.

And now it starts its head-polishing anew,
slicking and twisting. I'm transfixed.
A child again, staring through the hall window

that looked across the alley
into the bedroom of Zopher's daughter
as she unbuttoned her blouse, shucked off her skirt,

and stood in her nylon slip, illuminated
by the naked ceiling bulb, brushing
and brushing her black lacquered hair.

How I Became Miss America

There she is, Bert Parks is singing
and I am weeping as her gleaming teeth shine
through the wide-open window of her mouth.
When I grow up, I could be her.
Though I can't dance or sing
and girls fool enough to do dramatic
readings never win. But I've got time
and tonight my tears are hers,
falling like sequins down those lovely cheekbones.
I've just embraced the first runner-up,
who pretends to be happy for me,
sheaves of roses cradled, mink-trimmed cape
waltzed over my shoulders.
I'm starting down the runway.
My mother sips her highball.
My father leans back on the grease spot
his wavy hair has rubbed into the sofa.
We're six miles inland from Atlantic City
in a railroad apartment over Hy-Grade Wines and Liquors.
They worked all week selling Seagram's and cheap wine
and this is Saturday night. Summer. The windows raised
to catch whatever breeze might enter.
No one could predict that twenty-five years later
I'd be chanting *No more profits off women's bodies*
at the Myth California counterpageant
where Nikki Craft poured the blood of raped women
on the civic center steps, splashing
her ceramic replicas of Barbies:
Miss Used, Miss Directed, and *Miss Informed.*
And Ann Simonton, former *Vogue* model, posed as *Miss Steak*
in a gown sewn from thirty pounds of scalloped bologna
with a hot dog neckline and parsley garnish.
I'd just left my husband and come out as a lesbian.

My lover, in a tie and fedora, marched
with her poster, *Nestlé Kills Babies.*
That night we didn't need a moon.
From the minute my child fell asleep until we collapsed,
exhausted on her water bed, we made love
as one of Nikki's statuettes
in a glow-in-the-dark blue gown and tiara
watched over us, *Miss Ogyny*
painted in gold across her sash.

French Chocolates

If you have your health, you have everything
is something that's said to cheer you up
when you come home early and find your lover
arched over a stranger in a scarlet thong.

Or it could be you lose your job at Happy Nails
because you can't stop smudging the stars
on those ten teeny American flags.

I don't begrudge you your extravagant vitality.
May it blossom like a cherry tree. May the petals
of your cardiovascular excellence
and the accordion polka of your lungs
sweeten the mornings of your loneliness.

But for the ill, for you with nerves that fire
like a rusted-out burner on an old barbecue,
with bones brittle as spun sugar,
with a migraine hammering like a blacksmith

in the flaming forge of your skull,
may you be spared from friends who say,
God doesn't give you more than you can handle
and ask what gifts being sick has brought you.

May they just keep their mouths shut
and give you French chocolates and daffodils
and maybe a small, original Matisse,
say, *Open Window, Collioure,* so you can look out
at the boats floating on the dappled pink water.

Women Walking

"I'm fat and I'm old and I'm going to die," Dorianne says
as we're taking our after-dinner walk on the grounds of Esalen,
which are gorgeous, but not very big, so we tromp back and forth
up the back entrance road, past the parked cars to the compost pile
where we turn around and start back again.

Dorianne's smoking American Spirits
with an Indian in a feathered headdress on the pale green box,
packaged to make you feel they're organic, connected to the Native tradition,
bits of tobacco in a soft leather pouch offered to the gods
to ward off something—maybe the exact thing she's feeling now.

We're crossing over the arched wooden bridge, the river running under us
past a round redwood meditation hall neither of us has ever entered.
"I took a shower," she says, "and as I was drying I looked in the mirror.
Wouldn't it be enough to be just fat or just old or dying?"
We're passing through the garden now.

There's a wall of sunflowers, each splendid
full-seeded head fringed with yellow flames,
and on the wide lawn ahead the yoga class unfurls supple arms toward the sun.
The aroma of whole-wheat bread baking mixes with the scent of salt and kelp.
I say, "I've gained back the weight I lost, I've got my potbelly again.

Last week I asked Janet how much it mattered on a scale of one to ten.
She said seven. I thought she'd say two—or three at most.
So I waited a few days and broached it again.
'Maybe I'll cut out desserts,' I ventured, but she was reading about hive death
and raids on illegal aliens and lacing up her boots to go to work."

We're headed toward the baths. You're not allowed to smoke
past the bench halfway down, so Dorianne grinds her cigarette into the dirt
and shreds it as we stride along. When we get to the bottom of the incline,
we can smell the sulfurous fumes, the hot bliss I now connect with sinking

into those stone tubs, but we turn right around and keep on walking.

There are so many things to feel bad about, just in our two families alone,
but we don't talk about them now. I've cried so much this past year,
I just can't cry anymore. We're crossing the bridge again.
Someone has planted succulents along the edge of a stump
like a ribbon of green-petaled roses. Dorianne lights another cigarette

with a Bic she slips from her pocket. "I stole this," she says, "from the 7-Eleven."
"Oh," I say, "do you do that a lot?" She takes out a smaller Bic.
"This one I bought. My hair looks terrible, even though I washed it."
"I read," I tell her, "the average woman has 12.5 miles of hair."
"We get nervous with silence," she says.

"Mostly we talk just to reassure each other."
"Yeah," I say, "I'm not going to eat you. Don't eat me."
Dorianne slides her hand through my arm. There's not a star visible in the sky.
The fog's come in so thick we can barely see the tops of the cypress.

We've passed the compost again and are headed back down.
"Do you want to soak in the baths?" I ask. "No," she says,
"Joe's been down there already and he'll be back soon."
We're standing outside her door. She says, "To me, your belly is only a two."
"Probably not even that," I say and kiss her and go to my room.

Jazz

Today I'm thinking about this child's life—
the rags of it, the ragged waves of it, the vaporous
fumes of it, the split tree, stomped-out spark,
the one-eyed, peg-legged pirate of it, the overripe
kissed-to-bruises fruit, the exposed
negative, the burned-out-bulb marquee. And then
I start thinking maybe there's hope.
Maybe his life could be like jazz
that starts out with a simple melody,
nothing complicated, nothing jittery or twisted,
and then breaks off, kisses it, waves goodbye,
ripens the notes, tears the tune to rags,
strips it, pokes out an eye, burns it,
sends it up in smoky wreaths,
reaches inside and steals the honey,
bees streaming out in black ribbons,
and when it seems as though it's long gone, ashes and bone,
when it's strung out, wrung out, blasted
with a wrecking ball, bombed out, concrete dust,
it slides over and spirals up in one high thin note
stretched so far you can't tell if the ache
is bitter or sweet, it returns
to the melody, rinsed pure and clean of the past,
you almost can't bear it, the deliverance,
the song come home.

Cold

On this early morning in Vancouver, my son and I stop
on our way to breakfast when we hear
the Kenyan will soon be running past this corner.
Of course we want to see his gorgeous stride,
but after half an hour I'm shivering
in my thin sweater. That's when my son begins
to rub my back—offering up the heat of his palms.
What could be better than to stand here hungry
and be curried like this? If I hadn't been cold
I wouldn't have his hands on my spine,
flaring across my shoulder blades. For a moment
it seems possible that every frailty, every pain,
could be an opening, a crack that lets the unexpected
reach us. How can I remember this
when I'm old and need so much?

More

My mother-in-law can't cut her toenails anymore,
can't see to tweeze the hairs on her chin.
She's got enough of her mind to be aware
how much she's dimming every day.
What for? she says over and over.
But when I ask if she's really had it,
she says no, she wants another day.
She wants a new black sweater—and earrings.
I gave you all my good earrings, she says,
looking at me as though I'm going to steal
the gold out of her teeth.

Deceiving the Gods

The old Jews rarely admitted good fortune.
And if they did, they'd quickly add *kinahora*—
let the evil eye not hear. What dummkopf
would think the spirits were on our side?
But even in a tropical paradise
laden with sugarcane and coconut,
something like the shtetl's wariness exists.
In Hawaii, I'm told, a fisherman
never spoke directly, lest the gods
arrive at the sea before him.
Instead he'd look to the sky,
the fast-moving clouds, and say,
I wonder if leaves are falling in the uplands!
Let us go and gather leaves.
So, my love, today let's not talk at all.
Let's be like those couples
eating silently in restaurants,
barely a word the entire meal.
We pitied them, but now I see
they were always so much smarter than we were.

The Beginning of the End

When I was young and married, I kissed
another man. Afternoons, I'd hold the big
old-fashioned phone, his voice entering my body,
slipping through the dark passages of desire.
And while my baby crawled at my feet,
teething on a roll of Scotch tape, I'd jingle my keys,
whatever I could reach to keep her quiet.
I told him I'd go anywhere with him:
a beach on Tahiti, a phone booth in Detroit.
I thought it was the babysitter who walked in
the front door. I heard the refrigerator open,
the sucking sound of the seal pulled apart.
She was looking for the one Coke I bought her
each week among the armada of my husband's
vitamins, his alfalfa sprouts, the chopped garlic
and olive oil he mixed in his orange juice
to cleanse his liver, shuffling aside the stacks
of crushed-lentil patties and the salad dressings
he lined up like the seven pillars of faith.
When I heard footsteps in the hall, I turned—
and there he was, standing in the doorway,
bewildered, like an animal brought back
from extinction. *Papa,* my baby said,
chewing on the spine of a new book of poems.

Pleasantville, New Jersey, 1955

I'd never seen a rainbow or picked
a tomato off the vine. Never walked in an orchard
or a forest. The only tree I knew
grew in the square of dirt hacked
out of the asphalt, the mulberry
my father was killing slowly, pounding
copper nails into its trunk.
But one hot summer afternoon
my mother let me drag the cot onto the roof.
Bedsheets drying on the lines,
the cat's cardboard box of dirt in the corner,
I lay in an expanse of blueness. Sun rippled
over my skin like a breeze over water.
My eyelids closed. I could hear the ripe berries
splatting onto the alley, the footsteps
of customers tracking in the sticky purple mash.
I heard the winos on the wooden crates,
brown bags rustling at the throats of Thunderbird.
Car engines stuttered, came to life, and died
in the A&P parking lot and I smelled grease and coffee
from the diner where Stella, the dyke, washed dishes,
a pack of Camels tucked
in the rolled-up sleeve of her T-shirt.
Next door, Helen Schmerling leaned on the glass case
slipping her fist into seamed and seamless stockings,
nails tucked in, to display the shade, while Sol
sucked the marrow from his stubby cigar,
smoke settling into the tweed skirts and mohair sweaters.
And under me something muscular swarmed
in the liquor store, something alive
in the stained wooden counter and the pungent dregs
of beer in the empties, the shorn pale necks
of the deliverymen, their hairy forearms,

my mother greeting everyone, her frequent laughter.
The cash register ringing
as my parents pushed their way, crumpled dollar
by dollar, into the middle class.
The sun was delicious, lapping my skin.
I felt that newly arrived in a body
as the city wheeled around me—
the Rialto Theater, Allen's Shoe Store, Stecher's Jewelers,
the whole downtown three blocks long.
And I was at the center of our tiny
solar system flung out on the edge
of a minor arm, a spur of one spiraling galaxy,
drenched in the light.

The Morning After

You stand at the counter, pouring boiling water
over the French roast, oily perfume rising in smoke.
And when I enter, you don't look up.
You're hurrying to pack your lunch, snapping
the lids on little plastic boxes while you call your mother
to tell her you'll take her to the doctor.
I can't see a trace of the little slice of heaven
we slipped into last night—a silk kimono
floating satin ponds and copper koi, stars falling
to the water. Didn't we shoulder
our way through the cleft in the rock of the everyday
and tear up the grass in the pasture of pleasure?
If the soul isn't a separate vessel
we carry from form to form
but more like Aristotle's breath of life—
the work of the body that keeps it whole—
then last night, darling, our souls were busy.
But this morning, it's like you're wearing a bad wig,
disguised so I won't recognize you
or maybe so you won't know yourself
as that animal burned down
to pure desire. I don't know
how you do it. I want to throw myself
onto the kitchen tile and bare my throat.
I want to slick back my hair
and tap-dance up the wall. I want to do it all
all over again—dive back into that brawl,
that raw and radiant free-for-all.
But you are scribbling a shopping list
because the kids are coming for the weekend
and you're going to make your special crab cakes
that have ruined me for all other crab cakes
forever.

What Did I Love

What did I love about killing the chickens? Let me start
with the drive to the farm as darkness
was sinking back into the earth.
The road damp and shining like the snail's silver
ribbon and the orchard
with its bony branches. I loved the yellow rubber
aprons and the way Janet knotted my broken strap.
And the stainless-steel altars
we bleached, Brian sharpening
the knives, testing the edge on his thumbnail. All eighty-eight Cornish
hens huddled in their crates. Wrapping my palms around
their white wings, lowering them into the tapered urn.
Some seemed unwitting as the world narrowed;
some cackled and fluttered; some struggled.
I gathered each one, tucked her bright feet,
drew her head through the kill cone's sharp collar,
her keratin beak and the rumpled red vascular comb
that once kept her cool as she pecked in her mansion of grass.
I didn't look into those stone eyes. I didn't ask forgiveness.
I slid the blade between the feathers
and made quick crescent cuts, severing
the arteries just under the jaw. Blood like liquor
pouring out of the bottle. When I see the nub of heart later,
it's hard to believe such a small star could flare
like that. I lifted each body, bathing it in heated water
until the scaly membrane of the shanks
sloughed off under my thumb.
And after they were tossed in the large plucking drum
I loved the newly naked birds. Sundering
the heads and feet neatly at the joints: a poor
man's riches for golden stock. Slitting a fissure
reaching into the chamber,
freeing the organs, the spill of intestines, blue-tinged gizzard,

the small purses of lungs, the royal hearts,
easing the floppy liver, carefully, from the green gallbladder,
its bitter bile. And the fascia unfurling
like a transparent fan. When I tug the esophagus
down through the neck, I love the suck and release
as it lets go. Then slicing off the anus with its gray pearl
of shit. Over and over, my hands explore
each cave, learning to see with my fingertips. Like a traveler
in a foreign country, entering church after church.
In every one the same figures of the Madonna, Christ on the cross,
which I'd always thought was gore
until Marie said to her it was tender,
the most tender image, every saint and political prisoner,
every jailed poet and burning monk.
But though I have all the time in the world
to think thoughts like this, I don't.
I'm empty as I rinse each carcass,
and this is what I love most.
It's like when the refrigerator turns off and you hear
the silence. As the sun rose higher
we shed our sweatshirts and moved the coolers into the shade,
but, other than that, no time passed.
I didn't get hungry. I didn't want to stop.
I was breathing from some bright reserve.
We twisted each pullet into plastic, iced and loaded them in the cars.
I loved the truth. Even in just this one thing:
looking straight at the terrible,
one-sided accord we make with the living of this world.
At the end, we scoured the tables, hosed the dried blood,
the stain blossoming through the water.

Bottom Line

The birds are singing like crazy this morning.
Whistling and chirping, warbling, squawking,
claiming their territory, *mine, mine, mine,*
and calling for sex, pouring themselves
into the blue bowl of morning.
When Dan was hit by the wheel of a truck,
left dead from the neck down
except for one forefinger,
he made a bargain with God
that he'd live a year before killing himself.
By the end, he had weeping bedsores
and couldn't sit up in his wheelchair.
He made another deal that he'd stick around
only if he didn't have to live that way,
lying facedown on a bed, looking into a mirror
to see people. The following year
he had another bout of sores and a kidney infection
that put him in the hospital.
I was ashamed, Dan said, I didn't have a bottom line.
I wanted to live no matter what.

Ode to the Heart

heart let me more have pity on
Gerard Manley Hopkins

It's late in the day and the old school's deserted
but the door's unlocked. The linoleum dips
and bulges, the halls have shrunk.
And I shiver for the child
who entered that brick building,
his small face looking out
from the hood of a woolen coat.

My father told me that when he was a boy
the Jews lived on one block, Italians another.
To get home he had to pass
through the forbidden territory.
He undid his belt and swung it wildly
as he ran, wind whistling
through the buckle. Heart
be praised: you wake every morning.
You cast yourself into the streets.

Neighbor

When my kids were small
our neighbor yelled at her kids
who were old enough to yell back.
Every evening we'd have
Lyle, Lyle, Crocodile, followed by
Get out! Fuck you, you bitch!
My son's bedroom window
was a straight shot from their kitchen,
a natural place for fights to start.
Her vocal cords could herald gladiators,
vibrate the galleries of the Colosseum.
Sometimes I'd knock on her door
and tell her it had to stop.
You try talking to them, she'd say,
pulling me into the house
with her fat, foamy arm,
sitting me down at the kitchen table
across from her daughter, furious
hair flickering around her face,
and her son, slumped
into the hood of his sweatshirt.
Sometimes I just called the police.
But when her kids grew up and left,
she got a boyfriend. And late at night
when I hear her cry out,
I can't help but be happy for her.
She, who'd been so miserable and alone,
now thrown into the democracy
of the body's pleasure, set free.

Ode to Invisibility

O loveliness. O lucky beauty.
I wanted it and I couldn't bear it.
When I was a girl, before self-serve gas,
as the attendant leaned over my windshield,
I didn't know where to look.
I could feel his damp rag rubbing the glass
between us. Or walking from the subway,
even in my work boots and woolen babushka,
all those slouched men plastered to the brick walls
around the South End of Boston—
I could feel them quicken, their mouths
opening like baby birds. I was too beautiful
and never beautiful enough.
Ironing my frizzy hair on the kitchen table.
All the dark and bright creams to sculpt my cheekbones,
musk dotted on my hot pulses,
and that pink angora bikini that itched like desire
as I laid myself down under the gold of a sky we didn't yet fear.
Hello, my pretty. Your ankles were elegant,
your breasts such splendor
men were blinded by their solar flare.
These days, I'm more like my dog,
who doesn't peruse himself in the mirror,
doesn't notice the gray at his temples, though I think
it makes him look a little like Cary Grant in *Charade.*
I can trot along the shallow surf of Delray Beach
in my mother-in-law's oversize swimsuit,
metallic bronze and stretched-out so it bulges like ginger root.
On one side, that raucous ocean surging and plunging,
on the other, the bathers gleaming with lotions and oils.
I can be a friend to them all, even the magnificent young,
their bodies fluid as the curl of a wave.
I can wander up to any gilded boy, touch

36

his gaudy biceps, lean in confidentially. I'm invisible
as a star at noon, a grain of clear sand.
It's a grand time of life: not so close to the end
that I can't walk for miles along the pulpy shore,
and not so far away that I can't bear
the splendid ugliness of this disguise.

Ordinary Sex

If no swan descends
in a blinding glare of plumage,
drumming the air with deafening wings,
if the earth doesn't tremble
and rivers don't tumble uphill,
if my mother's crystal
vase doesn't shatter
and no extinct species are sighted anew
and leaves of the city trees don't applaud
as you zing me to the moon, starry tesserae
cascading down my shoulders,
if we stay right here
on our aging Simmons Beautyrest,
dumped into the sag in the middle,
that's okay.
You don't need to strew rose petals
in my bath or set a band of votive candles
flickering around the rim.
You don't need to invent a thrilling
new position, two dragonflies
mating on the wing. Honey,
you don't even have to wash up after work.
A little sweat and sunscreen
won't bother me.
Take off your boots, babe,
swing your thigh over mine. I like it
when you do the same old thing
in the same old way.
And then a few kisses, easy, loose,
like the ones we've been
kissing for a hundred years.

Ode to Boredom

We gathered firewood. We gathered walnuts
and cracked them on the stone wall, black hulls
staining our hands. Janet took a photo of Max and me
looking up from the shells. My hair blown across
my face. The wings of his small eyebrows raised
as if asking a question. Late afternoon,
the rose-washed light of southern Italy,
the month of December stretched out before us
like the rows of olive trees the pickers climbed
on homemade ladders, combing the silver branches,
bitter harvest falling to the nets spread beneath them.
We'd settled in a town near the heel
of the country, rented a crumbling conical house,
domed roof, stone slabs laid without mortar.
Nothing to do. Not a church or museum. Not even
a newspaper in English. We'd read all our books
and I'd embroidered the linen dishtowels.
We walked the empty vineyards and cherry orchards.
In the cold dusk, I carried Max, his arms around my neck.
A farmer poured acorns for pigs
that squealed and snuffled. A shaggy horse
stood in a muddy corral. Once
we watched his bright penis emerge.
We bought clay and a tin of watercolors,
fashioning a miniature sty, painting the pigs hot pink,
rice grains filling their trough. I was bored
for the first time since childhood.
One night we sat in the lobby of the only hotel,
watching cartoons in Italian. How the days opened,
space widening between the hours.
The world that had been rushing by so fast
slowed down, stopped. I stood still
in my bare feet, light falling through the doorway

at an angle that seemed never to change,
as though the low winter sun stretched out on the limestone
and fell asleep there.

Flies

The story goes that as a boy,
the great Polish writer Bruno Schulz
fed sugar water to the last houseflies of autumn,
giving them strength for the bitter winter.
And I read about another lover of *Musca domestica*
who with only a whistle and the force of concentration
taught one envoy to come to his desk.
It would orbit, then land on his wrist
with a minute impact. Then they could reflect together,
the insect with his complex eye, the man, his simple one.
I am a novice with many failures,
but if the day is cool enough I can capture
a compliant fly in clear glass,
all emerald thorax and buzzing wings,
releasing it into the afternoon.
And by night I've perfected a method
for shepherding strays out to the stars.
Starting with the farthest room in my home,
I extinguish the lamps one by one,
luring the flies from dark to bright.
When I reach the door with my small skein,
I illumine the porch light, open the screen,
and watch them sail out from the shadows
into the warm yellow current.

Moonlight

On the radio, Amer Shurrab
tells how his father and two brothers
were stopped in Gaza by Israeli soldiers.
Both brothers shot.
One dead on one side of the car.
One bleeding to death on the other.
Twenty hours lying in his father's arms
while the soldiers wouldn't let a medic through.
Maybe there shouldn't have been moonlight
shining on this man as he crawled
behind the car, driving off the feral cats
that stalked his son's body.
Maybe this is no place for the persistence
of the physical world. The moon
waxes full, glazing the crown
of the father's head, the planes and angles
of his sons' faces. Its reflection
strewn across the dark pools.

Ode to the Fish

Nights when I can't sleep, I listen to the sea lions
barking from the rocks off the lighthouse.
I look out the black window into the black night
and think about fish stirring the oceans.
Muscular tuna, their lunge and thrash
churning the water, whipping up a squall,
storm of hunger. Herring cruising,
river of silver in the sea, wide as a lit city.
And all the small breaths: pulse
of frilled jellyfish, thrust of squid,
frenzy of krill, transparent skin glowing
green with the glass shells of diatoms.
Billions swarming up the water column each night,
gliding down at dawn. They're the greased motor
that powers the world. Shipping heat
to the arctic, hauling cold to the tropics,
currents unspooling around the globe.
My room is so still, the bureau lifeless,
and on it, inert, the paraphernalia of humans:
keys, coins, shells that once rocked in the tides—
opalescent abalone, pearl earrings.
Only the clock's sea-green numerals
register small changes. And shadows
the moon casts—fan of maple branches—
tick across the room. But beyond the cliffs
a blue whale sounds and surfaces, cosmic
ladle scooping the icy depths. An artery so wide,
I could swim through into its thousand-pound heart.

Waiting for Rain

Finally, morning. This loneliness
feels more ordinary in the light, more like my face
in the mirror. My daughter in the ER again.
Something she ate? Some freshener

someone spritzed in the air?
They're trying to kill me, she says,
as though it's a joke. Lucretius
got me through the night. He told me the world goes on

making and unmaking. Maybe it's wrong
to think of better and worse.
There's no one who can carry my fear
for a child who walks out the door

not knowing what will stop her breath.
The rain they say is coming
sails now over the Pacific in purplish nimbus clouds.
But it isn't enough. Last year I watched

elephants encircle their young, shuffling
their massive legs without hurry, flaring
their great dusty ears. Once they drank
from the snowmelt of Kilimanjaro.

Now the mountain is bald. Lucretius knows
we're just atoms combining and recombining:
star dust, flesh, grass. All night
I plastered my body to Janet,

breathing when she breathed. But her skin,
warm as it is, does, after all, keep me out.
How tenuous it all is.
My daughter's coming home next week.

She'll bring the pink plaid suitcase we bought at Ross.
When she points it out to the escort
pushing her wheelchair, it will be easy
to spot on the carousel. I just want to touch her.

The World Has Need of You

everything here
seems to need us

Rainer Maria Rilke

I can hardly imagine it
as I walk to the lighthouse, feeling the ancient
prayer of my arms swinging
in counterpoint to my feet.
Here I am, suspended
between the sidewalk and twilight,
the sky dimming so fast it seems alive.
What if you felt the invisible
tug between you and everything?
A boy on a bicycle rides by,
his white shirt open, flaring
behind him like wings.
It's a hard time to be human. We know too much
and too little. Does the breeze need us?
The cliffs? The gulls?
If you've managed to do one good thing,
the ocean doesn't care.
But when Newton's apple fell toward the earth,
the earth, ever so slightly, fell
toward the apple.

The Last Week

I thought she would want to save me
from it, the stench and shame,
but in the last week of dying,
my mother let me change her diaper,
let me wipe her with a warm, wet cloth
and slide the sheet under her hips,
the flesh softening, bones widening,
gravity pulling her back to earth like fallen fruit.
I need to say how precise she was.
She had a rage for order, my mother.
In the store she wrapped half-pints of cheap gin
with the same care she gave to Chivas Regal.
She smoothed the glossy holiday paper,
folding the torn edge under, sharpening
the crease with her thumbnail,
tucking the ends into a humble origami.
I thought she'd cling to her dignity
but she seemed to forgive her body,
all its chaos and collapse,
or maybe it was a final ripening
of trust or love, abandon.
I'm not sure what to call it.

Morning

after Gwendolyn Brooks

The morning of her death she
woke fierce, some dormant force revived,
insistent. For the last time
I sat my mother up, shifted the loose mass
of her body to lean against me. Her dried-up
legs dangled next to mine, triumphs
of will, all the mornings she forced
herself to spritz cheap perfume,
hoist each pendulous breast into
its halter, place the straps in the old
ruts. We were alone, petals
falling from bouquets crowded
around us. I pulled
some pillows behind me when I couldn't
hold her any longer
and we rested there, the
body of my mother slumped
against my breast, the slow droop
of green stalks in their vases.
Her long-exhaled breaths
kept coming against her
resolve. And in the exquisite
pauses in between
I could feel her settle—
the way an infant
grows heavier and heavier
in your arms
as it falls asleep.

Walking by Circle Market Late at Night

The city is quiet
as though it cried itself out.
Circle Market, its windows busy
with stickers for surfboard wax and bands
with names like Make-A-Mistake,
is dark now too. Last year
the owner was held up,
but he handed over the money
and wasn't shot. The next day
I sealed two twenties and a ten
in an envelope and gave it to him.
We went there a lot
when the kids were little,
Popsicles and nights we ran out of milk.
Mr. Song on his high stool
by the cash register, presiding
over the aisles, the dusty cans
of Campbell's soup and Hamburger Helper,
Huggies and Ajax.
His body looked sunken
and his eyes jerked over to the door
when he told me the man pointed
a gun at his wife—she'd been sitting
on a stack of Sunday *Chronicles*—
and warned him not to reach
for the phone. After that
he wouldn't let me pay for my pint
of Häagen-Dazs and added
an ice-cream sandwich on top—
for the child he said, even though
the youngest is grown and gone.
When I protested he slipped in
a Snickers bar and when I insisted

he couldn't keep doing this,
he tossed in a box of Chiclets.
Last summer when my friend was visiting,
I sent her instead, but he'd seen us
walking the dog together
and wouldn't let her pay, either,
sneaking in a pack
of American Spirit lights and a yellow Bic.
The Greeks believed
every human act is perilous.
I can't go in there anymore.

Ode to the God of Atheists

The god of atheists won't burn you at the stake
or pry off your fingernails. Nor will it make you
bow or beg, rake your skin with thorns,
or buy gold leaf and stained-glass windows.
It won't insist you fast or twist
the shape of your sexual hunger.
There are no wars fought for it, no women stoned for it.
You don't have to veil your face for it
or bloody your knees.
You don't have to sing.

The plums bloom extravagantly,
the dolphins stitch sky to sea.
Each pebble and fern, pond and fish
is yours whether or not you believe.

When fog is ripped away
just as a rust-red shadow slides across the moon,
the god of atheists isn't rewarding you
for waking in the middle of the night
and shivering barefoot in the field.

This god is not moved by the musk
of incense or bowls of oranges,
the mask brushed with cochineal,
polished rib of the lion.
Eat the macerated leaves
of the sacred plant. Dance
till the stars blur to a spangly river.
Rain, if it comes, will come.
This god loves the virus as much as the child.

Restaurant

Before she told me, she let me
finish my dinner. I can still see
the pinkish cream sauce
blossoming on the china.
I didn't know yet if I could walk
when I pushed myself back from the table.
This is what gets me:
I didn't throw the stained dish against the wall.
I slipped the plastic from my wallet.
I signed my name.
No matter what we're up against,
no matter who just shot up an overdose
or broke his spine at the fifth cervical,
no matter that a child's in prison,
or turning tricks in another city,
very few people are dropping to all fours
and baying at the empty white plates.
How can you not love the human animal?
In every restaurant in Fresno, California,
the diners are opening
their cloth or paper napkins.
They spear a chunk of potato
and find as they always did
the opening to their mouth.
They chew. And they swallow.
They sip the icy water.

Prayer

Once I wore a dress liquid as vodka.
My lover watched me ascend
from the subway
like I was an underground spring
breaking through.
I want to stop wanting to be wanted like that.
I'm tired of the song the rain sings in June,
the chorus of hope, the ravenous green,
the earth, her ornate crown of trees
spiking up from her loamy head.
There are things I wanted, like everyone.
But to this angel of wishes I've worshiped
so long, I ask now to admit
the world as it is.

Boat, Vietnam

And there is a moment
eating bread and butter
on the Mekong River
when I taste the butter.

The sun has risen high enough
to make a bridge of light
over the muddy water.

There is no war here now.
And only the usual number
of people are dying.

Ode to Dr. Ladd's Black Slit Skirt

Praise to the little girl whose grandmother taught her to embroider,
slip the tip of the needle through the taut cloth and scallop the clouds,
fasten the feathers to bluebird wings.

And praise to the student who gulped muddy coffee
and memorized maps of muscles, puzzle of bones,
slid tendons through their shafts, curling and uncurling
each finger of the corpse like a deft puppeteer.

When I got to the ER Janet lay there, the morphine
not strong enough to blunt the pain.
Her arm looked like a carcass where a lion had fed.

Praise Dr. Ladd pulling green scrubs over her head
and gathering her long hair under a cap.

All the days we drove up to Stanford and waited for hours
in the room with the ugly orange carpet,
thumbing through tarnished pages of *National Geographic*,
wondering what Dr. Ladd would be wearing,
until we heard the strike of her high heels on the hallway linoleum,
distinctive as the first notes of Beethoven's Fifth.

Praise her hands that lifted Janet's hand, her fingertips brushing
the gnarled scars, flesh lumped like redwood burl.

Praise her for getting up early to outline her eyelids,
slick her lips. And praise to her blouses, the silk creamy
as icing on a cake, the generous buttons open
like windows in summer. And praise

her bracelets' coiled gold and her wide leather belts
encircling her waist like two strong hands about to lift her.
Praise to her earrings, little jangling tambourines,

and her perfume that braced us like a dry martini.

But most of all, praise to her slim black skirt
with the slit up the front so that when she sat down
and crossed her legs, the two panels parted like the Red Sea
and we were seized by the curve of her calves,
the faceted shine of her knees sheathed in sheer black mesh,
a riff of diamonds rippling up her thighs.

Soixante-Neuf

Yesterday, rooting in the rich recesses,
tending each ridge and furrow,
I thought how like two farmers we were,
digging and planting, each working
our own corner of the field.

Ode to the First Peach

Only one insect has feasted here—
a clear stub of resin
plugs the scar. And the hollow
where the stem was severed
shines with juice.
The fur still silvered
like a caul. Even
in the next minute
the hairs will darken,
turn more golden in my palm.
Heavier, this flesh,
than you would imagine,
like the sudden
weight of a newborn.
Oh what a marriage
of citron and blush!
It could be a planet
reflected through a hall
of mirrors. Or
what a swan becomes
when a fairy shoots it
from the sky at dawn.
At the beginning of the world,
when the first dense pith
was ravished and the stars
were not yet lustrous
coins fallen from the
pockets of night,
who could have dreamed
this would be curried
from the chaos?
Scent of morning and sugar,
bruise and hunger.

Silent, swollen, clefted life,
remnant always remaking itself
out of that first flaming ripeness.

The Muse of Work

If I could choose my Muse,
she'd have red hair, short, spiky,
and green cat-eye glasses with rhinestones at the tips.
She'd wear a sleeveless dress, ruffled
over shallow scallop-shell breasts.
Can you see how young she is?
I think she's the girl Sappho loved,
the one with violets in her lap.
When she opens the door,
the white flurry of spring sweeps in.
But I've been assigned the Muse of work.
She's a dead ringer for my mother,
sipping black coffee, scrambling eggs,
a cigarette burning in a cut-glass ashtray.
Then she opens the store. Amber whiskeys
and clear vodkas shine on wooden shelves,
bruise-dark wine rising in the slender necks.
She fills in gaps where she's made a sale,
each pint and half-pint in its slot.
The phone's ringing, she's repeating,
Good morning, Hy-Grade Liquors,
jotting down the order on a carboned pad.
What makes a thing beautiful?
She wears a dark jumper and a fresh blouse each day,
pats her armpits with talcum,
sweeps her lips with Cherries in the Snow.
She knows the pale sherry you crave,
sliding it into a brown bag, sized precisely.
There's the smell of newsprint and stale beer.
The cash register rings its tinny cymbal.
She steps out of the walk-in icebox
with a case of Pabst Blue Ribbon,
bumping the door closed with her hip.

There was something I needed, something
I wanted to ask her. But I had to wait.
Fifty years later, my mother dead,
when I search for the words to describe
a thing exactly—the smell of rain
or the sound a glass makes
when you set it down—I'm back there
standing in the corner of the store, watching her
as she takes the worn bills,
smooths them in her palm.

Cheetah

Even with my good binoculars
it's a buff-colored smudge in the distance.
A smudge that pivots
so the outline of an ear
becomes visible, briefly,
before it's consumed into the whole again.
That's it. And yet
it's as if the world unbuttoned her dress
and we can't get enough
of looking. This is happiness—
without the freight of happiness. Only
the machinery of our eyes
working so hard to speed through
the air thick with dust and sun,
through the tall, tangled grasses.
We're looking through a pinprick
in the universe, bound
to any aperture, no matter how small,
glad to be swallowed completely. Hunger,
thirst, the need to pee
all disappear. We're focusing
in now, our pupils opening. We're way past
past regrets, failures, promises,
sunk deep
into that bit of tawny fur.

Their Naked Petals

While Sophie lay in perfect symmetry
between death and life, I pictured Da Vinci's
Vitruvian man stretched within the hoop of existence.
Her blood was summoned out of her body and wheeled
through a mechanical angel that breathed
it back from the blue of night sky
to the iron red of oxygen. While she lay still—
a copy of herself—drugged beyond an eyelid's
flicker, a stray synapse firing, nothing
to waste a joule of strength,
I picked the tenderest string beans
on my son's farm, thick fringe hanging
under leafy awnings,
some green, some a purple deep
as the dyes of royalty.
When the pods are young, each is so slight.
We harvested for hours to fill a lug,
mounding the slender bodies as the sun blazed.
We dug up beets, rude lumps
the gophers inscribed with their incisors.
We carried melons against our breasts,
fragrant with sugar and time. We all know
one life is not worth more than another,
but who does not beg for mercy?
Who does not want to be the one
who slips through the fence
when the god on watch turns away to take a piss?
The phone in my pocket rang and rang,
and with each call the odds fell.
I was already sweating as I started in
on the black-eyed Susans. Rows so yellow
it seemed such brightness could not have ruptured
from the dun-colored soil.

Tolstoy gave us the scene: Levin walking the streets
the morning after Kitty says she'll marry him.
He's dazzled by everything he sees—children
on their way to school, pigeons flying from a roof,
a hand arranging cakes in a shop window.
How is it that fear can also burnish the world?
The flowers opened their naked petals, shivering
gold in the hot breeze. I cut
only the freshest, centers packed with florets.
I stripped the leaves from the stems,
set them in water. One bucket and then another.
As the day wore on, the heat mounted, the light slanted
into my eyes. All I could see was the shadow
of the jagged corolla, blinded as I was by a sun
that I, for a moment, understood was a mortal fire
that would have its own death.
I remember the tough hairy stems. I remember
the green stain on my hands.
I remember my son with his face in his hands, my hand
on his shoulder, the bare muscle of his arm, his hardened palms.
And while Sophie lay still, unknowing as dirt,
we kept on—the gleaming eggplant,
the humble cabbages, the scarves of heat.

Another Story

After dinner, we're drinking scotch at the kitchen table.
Janet and I just watched a *NOVA* special
and we're explaining to Dotty, her mother,
the age and size of the universe—
the hundred billion stars in the hundred billion galaxies.
How about the sun? she asks, a little *famisht* in the endlessness.
I gather up a cantaloupe, a lime, a cherry,
and start revolving this salad around the chicken carcass.
This is the best scotch I ever tasted, Dotty says,
even though we gave her the Maker's Mark
while we're drinking Glendronach.
We're specks, I say.
Dotty's glossy red fingernails clink against her glass.
It's disgusting, she says.
What is? I ask her.
All of it, she says, and looks around as if she might
find in the sink a way to express it.
Then, *Shopping for wedding dresses,* she says.
I look at her, waiting for more.
Of course I think of her marriages,
the first husband who gambled his paycheck the week they were married,
the second who wouldn't allow her lesbian daughters in the house.
And my own husband with two PhDs from Harvard
and not an atom of common sense.
They're all dead now.
Along with her twin sister who everyone said was the beautiful one
and her oldest friend who shtupped Marlon Brando
in a car outside the Actors Studio.
And Dotty's marching toward death, leaning on her walker.
And in zero time, we're speeding behind her.
So I fill our cups again, this time giving Dotty the good stuff,
and I do the thing humans have always done
in the campfire's yellow light. I tell another story.

The one when Janet and I were first lovers
and she found a baby bat in her chimney
and tucked it in her bra where it fell asleep between her breasts.
It wasn't until we sat at the table and I poured her a drink
that the bat stirred. Then she opened her blouse
like an origami sky and the bat flew out, a dark star
in the staggering universe.

When You Return

Fallen leaves will climb back into trees.
Shards of the shattered vase will rise
and reassemble on the table.
Plastic raincoats will refold
into their flat envelopes. The egg,
bald yolk and its transparent halo,
slide back into the thin, calcium shell.
Curses will pour back into mouths,
letters unwrite themselves, words
siphoned up into the pen. My gray hair
will darken and become the feathers
of a black swan. Bullets will snap
back into their chambers, the powder
tamped tight in brass casings. Borders
will disappear from maps. Rust
revert to oxygen and time. The fire
return to the log, the log to the tree,
the white root curled up
in the unsplit seed. Birdsong will fly
into the lark's lungs, answers
become questions again.
When you return, sweaters will unravel
and wool grow on the sheep.
Rock will go home to mountain, gold
to vein. Wine crushed into the grape,
oil pressed into the olive. Silk reeled in
to the spider's belly. Night moths
tucked close into cocoons, ink drained
from the indigo tattoo. Diamonds
will be returned to coal, coal
to rotting ferns, rain to clouds, light
to stars sucked back and back
into one timeless point, the way it was

before the world was born,
that fresh, that whole, nothing
broken, nothing torn apart.

Let's

Let's take off our clothes and fool around.
We can roll all over
like dogs off-leash at Lighthouse Beach. Let's rummage
through each other's body
like a Fourth of July blowout sale, pawing through the orgy
of tweed and twill, silk and sequins swirling up in flurries.
The Buddha says don't argue until it's necessary.
Let's shuck oysters,
wash them down with dirty martinis,
the table littered with pearly shell. We can fill
the bathtub and pretend we're looking out
at sunset over Tomales Bay. Your breasts
are lanterns flickering on the water.
Your hips are still California's golden hills.
This morning I opened an e-mail from Texas
that said I'm going to hell and you don't really love me,
but if I repent, though my sins be scarlet,
they shall be as white as snow.
Darling, it's good to know we have options
but for now let's get triplet Chihuahuas,
carry them around in patent-leather purses.
Drag your guitar out from under the bed
and sing "Rose of My Heart" again.
I'll hunt in the garage for my zills and coin-covered bra
and do the three-quarter shimmy down the skinny hall.
Let's not think about our children, miles away,
doing things we'd rather not know.
Haven't we carved enough statues?
You remember the meadow I rented for you.
You wanted it sunny and edged with trees.
I paid the old woman a hundred dollars
so I could lay you down under the sky's blue marquee.
The longer we're together, the less I can tell you.

But hasn't it been a long day?
The President of Infinite Sadness is sorry
she ever ran for office. She imagined
she'd be like those brawny angels
who lower you into the tubs of warm mud at Calistoga.
But monkeys are gorging on peanut butter
so science can prove fat makes you fat,
and the workers who grow roses in Ecuador
are poisoned so we can say it with flowers.
Tomorrow we'll write letters. We'll try harder.
We'll turn down the thermostat and bicycle to work
and you'll swish plastic bags in a sink of soapy water
where they float like the jellyfish they're mistaken for.
But tonight let's bring Bessie back for an encore.
Don't you want a little sugar
in your beautiful bowl?
Let's make some rain, let's invent skin,
give me your glorious, gorgeous, generous thighs.
The ghost of my mother's in the basement doing laundry,
offering the damp clothes that extra little shake.
Wouldn't she be happy
to hear us nickering and neighing?
Wouldn't she be happy to know
death is feeding elsewhere tonight?
I'll dust your eyelids with cinnamon
and braid those old feathers into your hair.
Morning will find us asleep on the roof,
our faces blank as the new day, just the mockingbird
in the neighbor's tattered palm
whistling a tune that sounds a little like a Persian raga,
that twangy sitar, raising the sun.

About the Author

Ellen Bass has published several award-winning books of poetry, including *The Human Line* and *Mules of Love*. Her poems have appeared in *The New Yorker*, *American Poetry Review*, *The New Republic*, *The Kenyon Review*, and many other journals. She coedited the groundbreaking anthology of women's poetry *No More Masks!* and her nonfiction includes the best-selling *The Courage to Heal*. She teaches in the MFA program at Pacific University.

Poetry is vital to language and living. Since 1972, Copper Canyon Press has published extraordinary poetry from around the world to engage the imaginations and intellects of readers, writers, booksellers, librarians, teachers, students, and donors.

WE ARE GRATEFUL FOR THE MAJOR SUPPORT PROVIDED BY:

THE PAUL G. ALLEN
FAMILY FOUNDATION

Lannan

THE MAURER FAMILY
FOUNDATION

NATIONAL
ENDOWMENT
FOR THE ARTS

WASHINGTON STATE
ARTS COMMISSION

Anonymous
John Branch
Diana and Jay Broze
Beroz Ferrell & The Point, llc
Janet and Les Cox
Mimi Gardner Gates
Gull Industries, Inc.
on behalf of William and Ruth True
Mark Hamilton and Suzie Rapp
Carolyn and Robert Hedin
Steven Myron Holl
Lakeside Industries, Inc.
on behalf of Jeanne Marie Lee
Maureen Lee and Mark Busto
Brice Marden
Denise N. and Corey K.
H. Stewart Parker
Penny and Jerry Peabody
John Phillips and Anne O'Donnell
Joseph C. Roberts
Cynthia Lovelace Sears and Frank Buxton
The Seattle Foundation
Dan Waggoner
Charles and Barbara Wright
The dedicated interns and faithful
volunteers of Copper Canyon Press

To learn more about underwriting Copper Canyon Press titles,
please call 360-385-4925 ext. 103

The Chinese character for poetry is made up of two parts:
"word" and "temple." It also serves as pressmark for
Copper Canyon Press.

The poems are set in Adobe Caslon Pro.
Book design and composition by Phil Kovacevich.

9 781556 594649